ONE HUNDRED WAYS
FOR A

Horse to Train

its Human

ONE HUNDRED WAYS
FOR A

Horse to Train

its Human

BY
Tina Bettison

ILLUSTRATIONS BY
Anna Gawryś

Hodder & Stoughton
LONDON SYDNEY AUCKLAND

Text copyright © 2005 by Tina Bettison
Illustrations copyright © 2005 by Anna Gawryś

First published in Great Britain in 2005

2

British Library Cataloguing in Publication Data
A record for this book is available from the British Library

ISBN 0 340 90862 9

Typeset in Baskerville by Avon DataSet Ltd,
Bidford-on-Avon, Warwickshire

Printed and bound in Great Britain by
Bookmarque Ltd, Croydon, Surrey

The paper and board used in this paperback are natural recyclable products
made from wood grown in sustainable forests. The manufacturing processes
conform to the environmental regulations of the country of origin.

Hodder & Stoughton
A Division of Hodder Headline Ltd
338 Euston Road
London NW1 3BH
www.madaboutbooks.com

Time and time again, I see a horse trying to communicate something to its human and the human just not 'listening'. The more I know horses, the more I realise it is not the human that does the training, despite what we might think! This book is dedicated to Penny, who has trained me well and has me right where she wants me! I would also like to thank Jester, Orita, Perdie and Gunner for their sterling contributions.

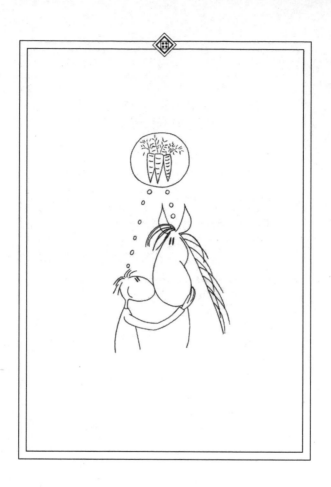

Contents

The Horse/Human Relationship

When a horse and a human come together in a relationship, it's a partnership, a never-ending dance. Teaching your human your language and training your human to dance with you can be incredibly rewarding. Unfortunately, there just might be a lot of treading on toes in the process!

A dult humans can be difficult to train. Patience, persistence, consistency, planning, co-operation and an ability to overcome setbacks and move on will all be important in your training programme, along with the belief that your human will get there eventually.

There will at some point be a tussle for the leadership position between you and your human. Humour them and allow them to think they are the boss while quietly watching them muck out your stable, fill your water buckets, pick out your feet and struggle to manhandle a barrow-load of horse pooh. Remember, they frequently work long hours in a job they hate just so that they can pay to do this in their spare time.

Children, like foals, are carefree and eager to learn and have fun. They tend to listen to you more intently than they listen to their parents, so you rarely have to repeat the lesson and you have the satisfaction of knowing you have got one over on the adults.

Stable Manners

If a human thinks that another human doesn't understand them, they usually keep saying the same thing but say it louder. If they don't hear our simple 'please move out of my space' message, expressed by a push with the nose, it is quite acceptable to launch at your human with teeth bared. If they don't hear that, then add in ears pinned back and eyes rolling. They'll get it then.

Humans often forget their manners when entering your personal space. Barging them should show them the error of their ways, particularly combined with standing on their foot or the eye-roll. While they are hopping about, they will have an opportunity to reflect on their rudeness.

If the human is throwing their weight around a bit, throw yours back and stamp slightly harder on their foot. If that fails, a quick turn on the forehand to present them with your backside followed by firing off both barrels should also give them the message that you are a little upset with their attitude and their invasion of your space.

Pawing and stamping are useful means of communicating that you want attention. Use the front foot pawing technique on well-manicured grass or the neat gravel driveway – humans detest deface-ment of these areas so will rush to your side to distract you.

On a concrete yard, a good paw creates a real racket and wears your shoes down nicely. If that doesn't bring them scurrying over to you, just scrape harder and louder, and if you are still ignored then the 'I'm a celebrity, pay attention to me!' stamp of all four feet accompanied by a loud and indignant snort should do the trick.

Feet are a really useful tool for training humans. Teach them to pick out your feet quickly and efficiently by refusing to hold your foot up for more than 10 seconds at a time. Doing small air circles

with your hind feet will ensure your human doesn't stay at that end longer than necessary. If all else fails, a swift sideways cow kick will get rid of the most barnacle-like human hanger-on.

For friendship, bonding and relationship-building, grooming is the key interaction with your human. They find it most endearing when you groom them and will spend hours grooming you back. If you can keep it up for long enough, they often forget they came to ride you.

Good grooming moves are lip twirling, particularly effective on the back of the neck, nibbling on the back of the legs, shoulders, arms and neck, and rubbing your head on any part of their body. Despite the tendency for them to fall over when you do this, they keep coming back for more!

Another good bonding exercise is gentle tugging at clothing. This is very satisfying, especially if you can find a bit of Velcro; for some reason humans love it when you pull the Velcro apart and they will spend hours sticking it back in place so that you can do it again. You may even be rewarded with treats for this trick.

Humans love soft muzzles. When you really want something, like a carrot or a treat or a day off, blow in their ear and gently nuzzle your soft nose against their cheek. This guarantees melt-down every time – they cannot resist it.

Walking in circles is a great tactic for avoiding rugs and tack. The longer you can keep your

human occupied with the tacking-
up process, the less time they will
have to ride. A particular favourite
is changing the direction of the
circle just as they have the saddle
poised for placing on your back.

The age-old head-up trick is also a good one for wasting tacking-up time. Always ensure you drop your nose into their hands and snuffle softly to pick up the bit. Then as they go to slip the bridle over your ears, swiftly lift your head and open your mouth. Unless they are 6ft 5in most humans cannot now reach your ears and the bit drops from your mouth. And so the process starts again.

Eventually your human may learn to tie you up outside the stable. This is an opportunity to try some other avoidance tactics. If your human takes your head collar off completely to put the bridle on, walking off can provide great entertainment. If they managed to get the reins round your neck, you will now be leading them all over the yard and if they didn't, they'll be following you around desperately hanging on to a bit of mane.

Having got the saddle on your back, some humans can be a little sharp at doing the girth up. A warning nip on their elbow should make them aware of this. However if becomes necessary to shout louder, a hefty bite on the bottom is the best method. Not only does it give them a clear 'Oi, that hurts!', it allows them to share in your discomfort (they like to share with you).

Safety on a lead rope: remind your human that monsters are everywhere and drag them away from potential danger to the nearest spot of sweet grass. Some will try to introduce you to the danger by attempting to lead you to it, and touch it to try to prove it is not a threat. They are mad and should be dragged back to the grass as soon as possible for their own safety as well as yours. If necessary mimic their madness by extreme eye-rolling.

Humans spend an extraordinary amount of money on the latest rugs with breathable fabric, integral neck cover, waterproofing and tog rates suitable for an Arctic sleeping bag. They adore this kind of retail therapy and find any excuse to do it. So satisfy their hunger for spending money on you by ripping your fieldmate's rug and encouraging him to rip your own.

A horse has to keep up its beauty regime and a mud-pack facial is ideal. The high-tech integral neck cover may keep the rain from running down your chest, but it won't

stop you from rubbing your face,
neck and mane in deep, cloying mud
while rolling. Humans love you to do
this: it means they can spend hours
trying to groom out the dried-up
clumpy bits at the end of the day.

All humans have different personalities and their own quirky behaviours and rituals. So it is worthwhile developing some quirks and rituals of your own to keep your human on their toes. For example: only stand quietly if your human puts your rug on in one movement from the off-side with no fiddling to get it straight. If they fiddle or put the rug on from the wrong side, then give them a full range of tail-swishing, making faces, nipping and fidgeting. If your human does things in the wrong order, give them a withering 'stupid creature' look, accompanied by an irritated tail swish.

Your human should always give you attention first, and preferably exclusively. If your human dares to fuss another horse in front of you, give them the turned-away, haughty-look-over-the-shoulder treatment or better still, shake like a leaf and refuse to be ridden.

Feeding time: it is only fair at the end of a long day of grazing and a short period of work that you are fed according to your nutritional needs. That means fed first, before your stablemates. Loud door-kicking and stamping should be enough to make your human scurry along with your food. They don't want to get a reputation for having the horse that kicks the door down at feeding time.

Treats: every time you do something good you should be rewarded. Encourage your human to carry a pocketful of treats at all times

and search their pockets at regular intervals. They find this quite endearing and will laugh at your antics. They will also reward you by giving you a treat, thus reinforcing that searching their pockets is a good behaviour.

Calling to your human when they come to the yard is a good ruse. They will go all soft and gooey because you recognised them and will give you a treat. Pampering your human's ego and appealing to their love for you ensures a steady supply of treats.

Humans work on the pain/ pleasure principle. If your human gives you what you want, even if you have been asking for it for weeks and they have only just worked it out, it is important to reward them. Let them know you appreciate them with a nose rub.

Sometimes your human will really irk or frustrate you and at these times it is best to avoid all contact with them (except at feeding time). This is easy if you are in your field. Just refuse to come anywhere near them, and avoid all their attempts at catching you by ensuring there is always at least half the field's distance between you.

In the stable, turn your bottom to them and refuse to look at them. Regardless of where they stand or how they approach you, present them with your back end. A carefully planned expulsion of wind at

just the right moment can be suffi-
cient to make them to leave you
alone.

Humans also respond well to
voice commands. Try these:

- Nervous whinny – use to tell your
  human you are not very confident about something
- Loud nervous whinny – use to tell
  your human you are very scared
- Fire-breathing snort – use to tell
  your human there is definitely a
  monster in that hedge and you
  need to get away from it fast.

Taking Your Human for a Ride

Mounting: steps are marvellous. You can have hours of fun moving away from them just as your human reaches the top step. A dance worthy of a 1920s ballroom will ensue: human stands on the steps, you move; human gets off the steps, moves them to where you are, mounts the steps, you move, and so on.

An alternative is the 'only stand still when alone' exercise. If your human enlists help, then try fidgeting, stamping and tail-swishing wildly until everyone lets go of you and moves away. Your human will eventually learn to trust you to stand still.

If your human is capable of mounting from the ground, then trot off as soon as one foot is in the stirrup and the other is in the air but not high enough to swing their leg over your back. They will soon learn to use a mounting block to avoid hanging under your stomach and trying to climb on at speed.

A final mounting exercise is the in-inhale/exhale method. Inhale while they are doing up the girth, and exhale while they are trying to get on so the saddle slithers round underneath you. A withering, surprised look from you is an optional extra.

B ucking can be a very expressive means of communication and one which many humans will not enjoy. An exuberant buck may just be showing your excitement, but not all humans will share your enthusiasm. This buck is best saved for the field when you are on your own – then you can really let rip.

The 'I'm in pain' buck is an entirely different matter. If having the human on board hurts, then get rid of them, and if the big buck is the only way of getting the message across, then so be it. They should have listened more carefully when you tried to draw attention to your discomfort in other ways.

Rearing as a communication tool should be used with care and only when your human appears to be completely deaf and all other methods have failed. This is the equivalent of shouting through a loudhailer.

Spooking is a highly versatile communication tool. Humans are often unaware of the monsters that lurk in postboxes, in hedges, and in certain places in the school. You need to educate them on these matters, particularly when you are really scared. After all, how will they

know how frightened you are if you don't tell them? A minor fright requires a jump sideways. A bigger scare can justify a jump and a spin. A really scary monster is definitely a cause for the spook, spin and run strategy.

S pooking can also be a method for gaining the attention of your human. If they have a tendency to let their mind wander while riding you, a quick spook at absolutely nothing is guaranteed to bring their focus back to you. You need to make sure that you continue to spook a few times in the same place, just so they think there really was something scary there.

Spooking may be used to avoid a command or instruction, or to get your own way. For example if you wish to canter and your human does not, a well-placed spook will throw them off balance and enable you to canter on for at least ten strides before they can get you back under their control.

Riding Activities to Do with Your Human

D epending on what you like to do, you may have to encourage your human to participate in certain riding activities. On no account tolerate an activity if you don't enjoy it. Life is too short.

Hacking

If your human does not like to hack, it will become obvious to you. They will spend a lot of time cleaning your tack, even when it is not dirty and hasn't been used.

They will groom you incessantly –
in fact you may start to go bald.
They will often drink a lot of coffee
and spend hours 'talking' horses,
but not actually riding.

If you like a change of scenery
every now and again, and enjoy
wandering leafy lanes, but your
human doesn't, you may need to
show them that you have no natural
survival instinct at all. Be happy to
plod merrily through heavy traffic,
past plastic bags (flapping or still),
farm machinery, barking dogs, party
balloons, puddles and any other
potential menace that they will be
terrified of.

In the early stages of training, you may need to endure their clinging, crying and attempts to get off. These are best dealt with by sighing and an expression which says 'what bag?' Eventually they will get used to most 'menaces' and will actually start to relax. It may take a while and much patience on your part, but at least you get out of the yard.

If you both like to hack, then you can look forward to many pleasant hours wandering about aimlessly, punctuated with the occasional good gallop. Your human will enjoy a good rub down from you afterwards, as a reward for being such a wonderful companion. This process also cleans the slobber from your chin.

If, however, you are an unhappy hacker yourself and you prefer the privacy of your field, then persuade your human that anything outside the yard gate is just too scary for words. All communication tools can be used to great effect before even leaving the yard. Spinning and low rearing combined with wild eye-rolling and nervous whinnying should be enough to persuade them to stay at home.

Your unhappily hacking human may persevere because, although they are terrified of going out, they are equally terrified of what other people will think of them. If so, you may have to give them a really good reason for staying at home. At every possible opportunity jump sideways, spin round and canter up the road. However, ensure that you are as sweet as pie when ridden in the school, so they don't decide to sell you.

Dressage/flatwork

Dressage is for divas of any shape or size. It doesn't matter whether you look like a supermodel, you

are a supermodel inside and that's what counts! So remember to be-have like one. Refuse to get out of bed unless the price is right – half a dozen carrots, a new hairdo, a posh frock and those lovely impractical white boots you have been coveting.

'Submission' is a key word in dressage. It's all about attention, confidence, harmony and lightness. You may have to work hard to train your human to submit to you. They frequently have a short attention span, their mind is elsewhere and they are rarely as confident as you would like them to be. Hence, you can't achieve the level of harmony you strive for. On no account should you submit to your human until they have done it first. This could take years.

'Impulsion' – the desire to move forward, elasticity of the steps, suppleness of the back and engagement of the hindquarters – is another key word. Your human's impulsion can be improved by chasing them. Sometimes just a menacing look is enough to dramatically increase the elasticity of their steps.

The rider's position, seat and balance are just as important for your comfort as for the judge's marks. To ensure your human learns to stay in balance with you and has a secure seat, catch them off guard

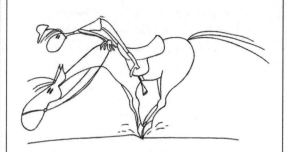

occasionally. The sudden head-down
trick with a lung-clearing snort is
useful here, as is the short sharp
spook at nothing in particular.
A head-between-the-knees bouncy
canter can be very effective too.

Correctness of the aids: this is where your human should give you a precise instruction as to what to do next – walk, trot, canter, etc. If you are a schoolmaster, then you simply refuse to do anything unless your human gets the aid right. For less experienced horses, the 'I'm simply confused' training method can be employed: i.e. you just do what you wanted to anyway and pretend that's what you thought you were being asked for.

Dressage involves a number of paces and the more advanced you get, the more paces you have to develop. You can practise *piaffe* (a trot on the spot) and *passage* (a very slow trot with lots of bounce) at every opportunity, whether asked for or not. While your human is trying to mount is a good time, or at any time when they want you to stand still.

As you progress you will need to train your human to do collected, working, medium, lengthened and extended walks, trots and canters, not to mention pirouettes. Leading your human is a good opportunity to practise these paces, and inadvertently stamping on their foot can be very effective in training for the pirouette.

The square halt: to avoid this simply move one foot forwards, backwards or sideways as soon as you stop. And then smile.

On the bit: this infamous phrase describes how you should accept the bit in your mouth, with the correct bend in your neck and your nose on a vertical line. If you don't enjoy dressage, then simply refuse to keep your nose on the vertical.

Sometimes if you seem a bit fresh, your human will decide to lunge you before riding. In their mind allowing you to run around them in circles on a long line is good because you can be free to buck and leap if you feel so inclined. Once they climb aboard you can refuse to do any more work because you are now tired from running round them in circles.

Jumping

As with the unhappy hacker, you may have a human who wants to jump but is scared of doing so. They love the thrill after they have done it, but the anticipation turns them into quivering wrecks. The

first thing you need to do with this human is to train them to hang on to your mane, not to your mouth. Refuse to jump anything unless they have let go of the reins completely, even if this means you depositing them on the floor.

O nce you have your human keen to jump, make use of any opportunity to do so. Insist on jumping the poles on the ground they are trying to get you to trot over, or the whip that's lying on the floor, a puddle; anything to get them used to leaving the ground.

H acking is a good opportunity to find obstacles. Take your human down ditches and up banks, wade through large puddles, jump over tiny ones, and seek out fallen logs to jump. All these things are good training for when you decide to take your human on a cross-country course.

M ost humans will have a fence they don't like. They usually blame you – 'he doesn't like spotty poles' – while you really don't care one way or another. You will know which fence this is as your human will kick harder and hold the reins tighter than at any other fence. If they don't want to jump it then it is only good manners to oblige them. If they want to jump it on their own, that's their choice.

Occasionally your human might encourage you to free jump at liberty in the school. Regardless of high the fence is, make sure you jump well over the height of the wings. This proves how fantastic you are, and that you can jump anything if you choose to.

Tight turns, jumping on an angle and jumping at speed are all skills you need in order to be a good competitive jumper, so you should practise them at every opportunity whether or not your human asks you to. That gate to your field can be an excellent training jump if your human seems less than keen to practise with you.

At some point in your jumping career, you will need to employ the Harrier Jump Jet method, where you take off from a standstill. This technique is useful when your human isn't sure whether they want to jump or not and then decides at the last moment to go for it. A few 'Harrier' jumps and your human will soon learn to make their mind up before the fence rather than at it.

If your human's ego gets a little out of proportion and you have to remind them who is boss, choose your fence carefully and never, ever give any indication of your intention to do anything other than jump it. Stride into the fence and then stop and spin sideways. Your human may or may not stay with you. It is vital that you then look completely incredulous and feign terror of the fence.

At some point, if you have aspirations to jump round Burghley, you will want to test your human's bravery and suitability for cross-country jumping. A nervous human is not necessarily a write-off and a gung-ho one does not always make the grade. A sensible, intelligent, level-headed human is best and if yours is not developing as you would like, you may want to trade them in for a more suitable jockey.

Seeing the stride is vital when jumping. Often your human will be seeing a different stride from you, in which case you need to ignore all their hauling about and show them you know best. Do not let them interfere in your job –after all, you don't tell them how to run their board meetings.

Human interference is particularly prevalent on the cross-country course. There you are, bounding along with a fence nicely coming towards you, and they start the slow-down fiddle, as if you didn't know the fence was there. It is wise to slow up enough to make your human feel listened to and to keep their confidence in you, but not enough to lose the impulsion to take the fence in your stride.

Getting humans used to certain cross-country fences is like getting them used to hacking – use lots of repetition and reward them for good behaviour. Jumping into, and trotting through, deep water, for example, can be very scary for your human. If necessary, take another experienced human along with you to show them how it's done. You might as well take along an equine mate to keep you company and have a laugh with at the same time.

$\mathcal{O}utings$

Your human will like to take you out to show you off at venues other than home. Your human will seem more stressed than usual in the lead up to and at these events, so it is your responsibility to bring some humour to the proceedings and lighten the situation. Here are a few ideas . . .

Turnout – how clean and pretty you look – will be important to your human. They will spend hours the day before washing your coat and tail, whitening your socks and adding sheen wherever they can. To take their mind off the competition, during the night take your rug off, create a large pooh and roll in it. Make sure you work it well into any white areas.

Your human may wish to plait your mane and tail. Try to entertain your human while they do this by swishing your tail and nodding your head in time to the music

they will inevitably have playing on
the yard to calm their nerves.

P laits are time-consuming to put
in but very easily shaken out. It
is important to test whether these

plaits will last the day. Just as your human has finished them and is admiring their handiwork, go for a full-on whole body shake and see what happens. If that doesn't move them, wait until your human has gone to check the transport and then rub your neck vigorously on the stable door frame.

Similarly, you can check the stability of your tail plait by rubbing your bottom along the wall. It would be tragic to get all the way to the event and find it had dropped out.

If you ever have a desire to pull off a shoe, now is a good time. If your human is a nervous wreck about this event, they obviously can't be that keen on going, so a lost shoe may be just the excuse they need to back out.

Eventually the moment will come when your human will try to walk you into a large black hole on wheels. If you are a seasoned traveller you may enjoy being taken for a ride, in which case you should bound up the ramp at great speed. Your human will be impressed by your enthusiasm (when their feet

are back on the ground again) and
doubtless a treat will come your
way.

Y ou may not like travelling
under horsepower other than
your own and you may need to make
your feelings clear. If possible, just
do not go near the ramp. Run backwards, circle, and drag your human
to the grass – anything to avoid the
approach.

If several humans surround you and there is no clear exit, place one foot on the ramp and lean back into a full body stretch with your head in the air, snort and then attempt to back up. You can lure them into a sense of false security by putting both front feet on the ramp, lift a back leg as if you are going forward then, just as they relax and think it is in the bag, run backwards or jump sideways so they have to start all over again.

At the competition venue, take a good look round to check out the opposition. Having tolerated the wobbly lorry and the second bath in two days, you want to be sure you stand a chance of winning a rosette. Despite what others say about 'it's the taking part that counts', it's not. You want to win.

The warming-up area is your chance to show off and psych-out the other competitors. Show them your best arabesque, tail-up *piaffe* and *passage*, with a couple of canter pirouettes thrown in for good measure, particularly if it's just a low-key local show. This should destroy the self-confidence of every one in the area, including your human.

Catching the eye of the judge is critical; you really want to impress them. Again, the tail-up *piaffe* works well, as does an enthusiastic 'look at me' buck, or a 'come on, dance with me' turn on the haunches while waving at the crowd with your front feet.

There will be one other opportunity to play to your public – the post-presentation lap of honour. Whether you got a rosette or not, your rightful place is at the front, leading the field.

Young Life – Foals and Families

The moment you open your eyes as a newborn foal, you start the process of teaching your human family. The first lesson you teach them is adoration. They will be totally smitten by you, as they are by all baby things. Your first wobbly steps are the ideal opportunity to encourage oohs and aaahs.

Encourage them to get to know you by playing. Foal games involve nipping and barging, mock-fighting, spooks, spins and mad dashes. All of these games prepare your human for survival skills they'll need later on.

Games will also help you find out if your human is a natural leader who may need to be kept in check, or a natural follower who may need encouragement and confidence-boosting. They will also start to learn the social skills necessary for being in your herd.

Grooming is an important part of establishing the relationship, or pair bond, between you and your human. So take a breather and groom them. They will delight in this and groom you in return. Once a good bond has been established, you will be able to attach a lead rope to your human and take them for a walk.

Life as the Family Pony

As the family pony, you may not just have one human to train – you may have a whole herd. This will certainly take some management on your part as they will all be at different stages of training and interest in you.

Lead stallion (Dad): he will be long-suffering with deep pockets which are usually empty as his mare and youngsters will continually raid them to buy things for you. He doesn't need training; Alpha Mare has done it for you.

Alpha Mare (Mum): she will probably look after you, even though that is supposed to be the youngsters' job. Don't even try to train her; she is Alpha to you (and every other living being).

Colts and fillies: you can train youngsters just as you would foals – lots of play, lots of rewards and a good kick when they forget their manners. However be prepared to deal out much love, cuddles and emotional sticking plasters if they don't come home with rosettes and ribbons from the local gymkhana.

M ost human herds also include a dog, which does bizarre things like eat your pooh and run off with your grooming brushes and bury them in the muck heap. The youngsters will roll around with this beastie and in fits of giggling, allow it to lick their faces – yuck!

O ne advantage of being the family pony is access to a varied diet. Make your great escape through the field fence to sample the family garden and herbaceous border. A good time to do this is when the family are asleep – then you won't be disturbed.

Mum may use manure from the muck heap to put around the roses. So while you are chewing on her prize dahlias, save her a trip and pooh on the roses directly.

Being able to win at gymkhana games is a very important role for the family pony, so practise your speed weaving, tumble turns and gallop to halt at every opportunity. It is useful to have some obstacles to practise around and you will find more of these in the carefully-designed garden than you will in your field.

Even tiny tots still on the lead rein can be taught the joys of gymkhana games. The little tot will squeal with delight! Mum's squeals may be for a different reason.

As soon as a tiny tot can hold a brush, they will try to use it on you, copying their elder siblings' behaviours. Your feet and knees will become very clean as this is the only area they can reach.

There is nothing youngsters love more than a game of hide and seek, and you can join in. Good places for you to hide are the shrubbery, the neighbour's shrubbery, anyone's garden shed, the bus shelter down the road, and behind the hedge in your field (on the outside of the field, of course).

Pony Club Camp, aka the Family Pony's Annual Conference (FPAC), is where you and your little colts and fillies get to play big time with other family ponies and their herds. In fact it is just one big mad herd of horses and humans staying up late, prancing, dancing and playing games – 'dump your child' is the favourite among the ponies.

The FPAC and pony club rallies are the best training ground for young humans and a great opportunity for family ponies to compare training notes and methods, pick up tips and share experiences.

The FPAC also provides an opportunity for you and your youngster to try new disciplines: e.g. long-distance riding (where you trot

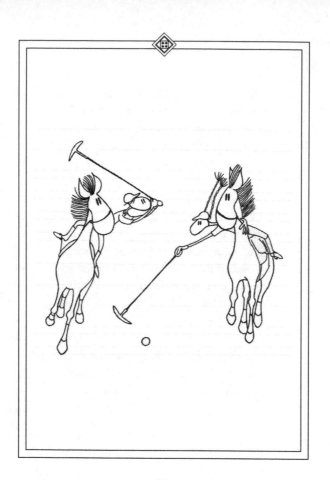

on and your youngster can't stop you for several miles), polo (you run up and down looking for a mint with a hole for your youngster to pick up with a stick) and racing (just an excuse for a flat-out gallop).

At the end of a long day's training you have the satisfaction of happy little humans hanging round your neck with undying love and gratitude, burying their little heads in your fur coat and pleading, 'Please can I sleep with Willy Wonty Buckmeoff, please, Mum, please?'

And you can smile to yourself, safe in the knowledge that you have done a good job and there are extra carrots in your feed bucket.